KNEES+
FURTHER ADVENTURES IN KENDAMA

By
The Void & Donald Grant

Illustrated by
Donald Grant

Published by
Butterfingers Books

Copyright ©2011

ISBN 978-1-898591-22-1

Copyright ©2011 The Void & Donald Grant

All rights reserved

First published 2011

Reprinted 2012

No part of this book may be reproduced without prior permission of the publisher

ISBN 978-1-898591-22-1

Layout and typesetting by TLMB

Published by Butterfingers Books

Also by the same author
"Spike! Mastering the kendama"
ISBN 978-1-898591-21-4

CONTENTS

Introduction & Anatomy	4	Gunslinger to Balance	32
History	5	Lighthouse Baseball	33
Grips & Stance	6	Mini Whirlwind	33
Swap and Pop	7	Cross-arm Turnovers	34
Drop and Pop	8	1 Hand Fork Cradle	35
Slam and Pop	8	Gammon Trap	36
Swing to Candle	9	Jumping Stick Cradle	37
Candle to Lighthouse	9	Double or Nothing Cradle	38
Candle to Balance	10	Stigmata	39
Nose Balance	11	Extended Tap-backs	40
Axle Spin	11	Double Tap-back	40
Pinkie Poke	12	Under Tap-back	41
Thumb Trap	12	Stopover	41
Fork Catch	13	Switch-hand Stopovers	42
Bat	13	Stopover Tap-back	43
Bat Exits	14	Around The Triangle	44
Bat Turn & Bird Turn	15	Hanging Swing In	45
Falling Down	16	Hanging Triangle Lighthouse	46
Tap In	17	The Drill	47
Build The Lighthouse	18	Sideways Drill	48
Faster Than Lighthouse	18	Fishing	49
Lighthouse Somersault	19	Landing Strip	50
Reverse Swing In	20	C-Whip	51
Reverse Aeroplane	21	Elbow Drop	52
Reverse Earth Turn	22	Mini Suicides	53
Jumping Stick Orbit	23	Suicide Swing In	54
Captain Hook	24	Fast Hand Base Cup	55
Tomahawk	25	Fast Hand Lighthouse	56
Jumping Tapback	26	Fast Hand Falling Down	57
Nodding Off	27	Orbit The World	58
Sisyphus	27	One And A Half Times Two	58
Swing Backhand Slip-on-stick	28	Around the U.S.A.	58
Rolling Around	29	Speed Trick B	59
Rumble Strip	29	Around Tunbridge Wells	60
Whirlwind Big Cup	30	The Last Word	64
Gunslinger Swing In	31		

INTRODUCTION

Welcome to "**Knees!**".

This book is intended as a sequel to our first book "Spike! Mastering the kendama", but we've also included a quick refresher course in the basic kendama techniques. You'll find this volume packed to the gills with new ideas, techniques, sequences and of course tricks. Both Eastern and Western influences are prevalent throughout, which is hopefully indicative of kendama popularity spreading across the globe.

Where we know it, we have also included the Japanese name of the trick. (Many thanks, again, to Matt Hall for the translations).

Read on, flex those knees, and catch downwards!

- The Void and Donald Grant, March 2011

ANATOMY

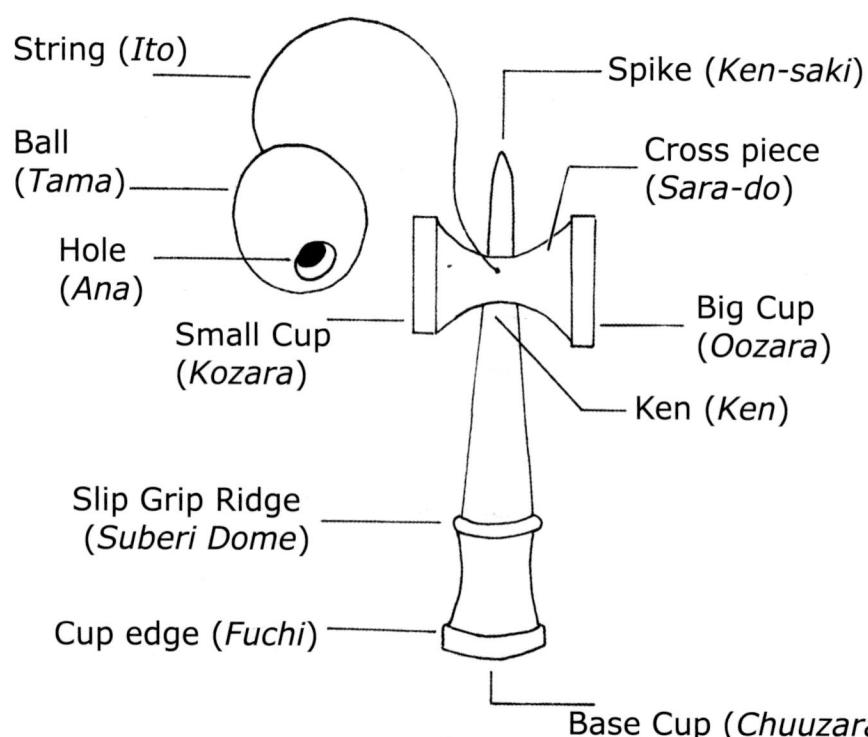

A kendama, strung right-handed

HISTORY

The very early history of kendama evolution is uncertain, but we can be sure that various cultures have developed their own versions of an "object catching" game.

It is thought that the basic *Cup-and-Ball* game in Europe was developed from a simple drinking game involving a cork, or ball of string, tied to a goblet or glass.

It was the French who evolved the *Cup-and-Ball* into a *Bilboquet*, by drilling a hole into the ball, and adding a spike to the body, to make a more interesting challenge. It was a craze in France in the 16th century, with king Henri III being a noted enthusiast.

In 1919, a Japanese artisan added a cross-piece with extra cups, and called it *Sun-and-Moon Ball*, after the shapes of the ball and the cups. The name was later changed to *Kendama*.

In 1975 the *Japanese Kendama Association* was formed to standardise the models of kendama, and to spread its popularity as a sport, via competitions and the introduction of beginner and advanced grades, similar to martial arts belts.

Late in the first decade of the 21st century, kendama began to take off as a craze in the western world amongst skaters, skiers and jugglers.

As for the future..... who knows?

"Cup-and-Ball"

Early drinking game?

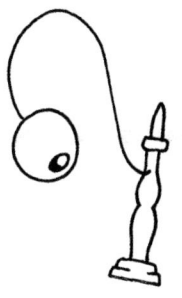

"Bilboquet", from France.

Mexican "Balero" or Venezuelan "Perinola"

Native American "Ring & Pin" game

The modern "Kendama"

It's written by the victors

GRIPS AND STANCE

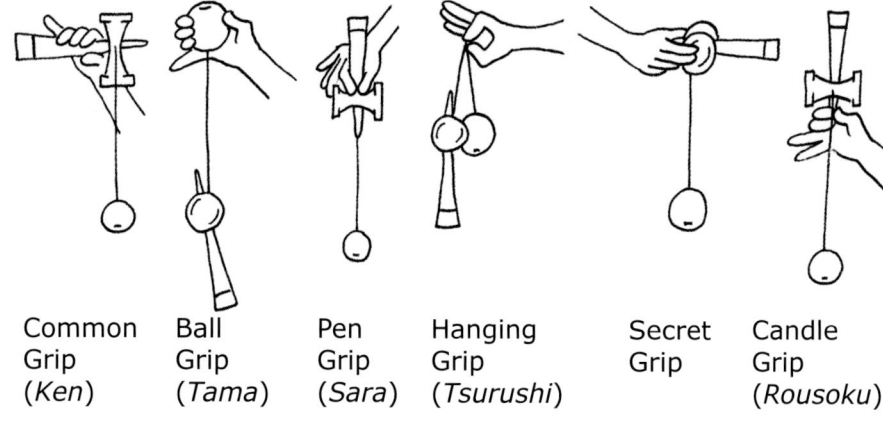

Common Grip (*Ken*) | Ball Grip (*Tama*) | Pen Grip (*Sara*) | Hanging Grip (*Tsurushi*) | Secret Grip | Candle Grip (*Rousoku*)

When playing kendama you should stand with your **Knees!** slightly bent and your feet about shoulder width apart. Your dominant foot should be placed a little forward of the other. It's important when playing kendama to use your entire body to make the pull up to catch, and because of this a proper stance can really improve your kendama play.

Big Cup (Oozara / 大皿)

Start with your knees bent, and the ball hanging centrally. Straighten your legs sharply as you pull upwards to make the ball fly up to about chest height. As it rises, scoop the ken underneath and close to the ball, making sure the cross piece is vertical. Bend your knees and lower your hand to make the catch. Try to 'cushion' the catch, rather than letting the ball 'hit' the cup.

Spike! (Tomeken / とめけん)

Start with the ball hanging between your knees, and sharply straighten your legs as you pull up. It is important to make sure your upwards pull is directly along the line of the string, as any sideways motion will make the ball rotate as it rises, which makes the catch very difficult. As the ball flies upwards, scoop the ken just underneath it, making sure you keep it completely vertical. Rather than stabbing the ken upwards, just sink your knees and let the ball fall onto the spike. Try to visualise the line of the string extending below the ball, and place the ken onto this imaginary line.

Refresher course

Swap and Pop
(Mochi Kaeshi Oozara/持ち変えし大皿)

Grip: Common Grip

We'll be nice, and start off the new book with a trick that's quite simple in execution, but surprisingly effective in appearance.

From either a big or small cup catch, pop the ball up and let it fall, while swapping the ken over to the other hand.

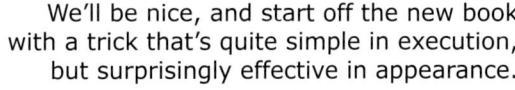

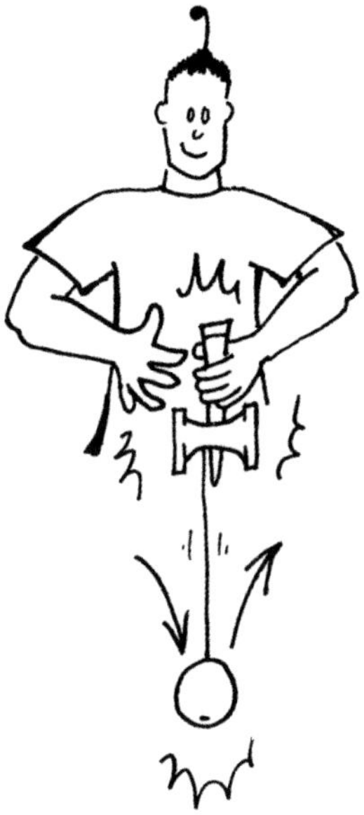

Now pull the ball back up to a cup catch in the other hand. (If you rotate the ken during the pass, the ball will come back to the same cup).

Tip
Bend the knees to avoid the ball hitting the end of the string with a jerk, which will make it come back up with a nasty spin.

Pop 'till you drop

Drop and Pop
(Mochi Kaeshi Chuuzara/持ち変えし中皿)

Grip: Ball -> Common Grip

What to do when you've landed an Aeroplane? Drop and Pop! Release your grip on the ball completely, letting the whole kendama start to fall through your hand. But then grab the ken on the way down, base cup still skywards. Let the ball fall to the bottom of the string, but then pull it straight back up and catch in the base cup. As ever, use your knees to soften the catch.

Slam and Pop
(Tomeken Otoshi Chuuzara/とめけん落とし中皿)

Grip: Pen Grip

Similar to Drop and Pop, but from a spike catch in pen grip (eg Stabbing Heaven).

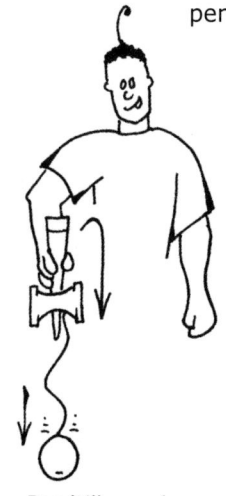

Not very tricky, but quite dynamic, and non-kendama types seem to like it!

Pop 'till you drop

Swing to Candle
(Mae Furi Rousoku/前ふりろうそく)

Grip: Candle Grip

Begin with the ken in the Candle Grip, with your other hand holding the ball pulled back towards your body.

Release the ball, bend and then straighten your legs. This will send the ball swinging upwards in an arc.

Bend the knees again to catch on the base cup.

Candle to Lighthouse
(Rousoku Mochi Toudai/ろうそく持ち灯台)

Grip: Candle -> Ball Grip

From the Candle, make a big dip, and straighten up. Release the ken with some sideways rotation, so that it starts to spin around the ball.

Candle work

Catch the ball in the Ball Grip, then focus your eyes on the base cup.

Try to catch the base cup on the ball *just before* the ken has reached vertical.

If you leave the catch too late, the rotation of the ken will topple it out of the Lighthouse balance, rather than *into* the balance.

Antidote
Now can you reverse the procedure, and go from Lighthouse back to Candle? It's much harder than you'd think!

Candle to Balance
(Rousoku Baransu/ろうそくバランス)

Grip: Candle Grip

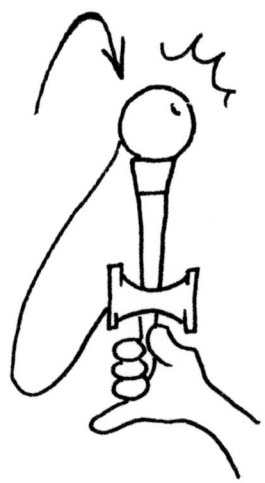

In a standard Candle Grip, the tip of the spike is usually resting gently on the side of the ring finger.

Why not try releasing your grip with thumb, index and middle fingers, and going into a dynamic balance with the whole Candle balanced on your ring finger?

Exit by gently hopping everything up, and catching the ken in a Pen Grip.

Candle work

Nose Balance (Hana Baransu/鼻バランス)

Grip: -> Common Grip

Lift up a loaded ken, and place it gently on the tip of your nose. Let go, and try to keep it there, balanced, for a few seconds.

To exit, pop the kendama up, using your legs to 'throw' it off the nose, and catch the whole shebang on its way down.

Variation
How about a nose balance of a Candle?

Axle Spin (Chuuzara Mawashi/中皿回し)

Grip: Non-standard

Grip a loaded ken by the base cup, as shown.

Now give a sharp twist with your thumb and middle finger, releasing the ken into a spinning balance, resting on your index finger.

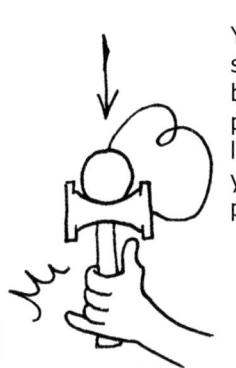

You'll only manage short spins at first, but with a bit of practice, they'll last longer than you first thought possible!

Tip
Push up for the launch, and sink down for the catch.

In the balance

Pinkie Poke (Koyubi Hime/小指姫)

Grip: Common Grip

Start as you would for a Spike, but extend your little finger, and catch the ball on your Pinkie.

From there, exit by flipping the ball off your finger onto any of the cups or, with exactly 1 spin, onto the spike.

Variations
Swing In to the catch.
How about a Pinkie Earth Turn?

Thumb Trap (Hittsuki Mushi/ひっつき虫)

Grip: Ball Grip (modified)

From a Ball Grip, roll the ball slightly along your thumb, to leave the pad of the thumb free.

Pull up as for a Lighthouse, but as the cross-piece comes level with the ball, trap the big cup against the side of the ball by pulling it inwards with your thumb.

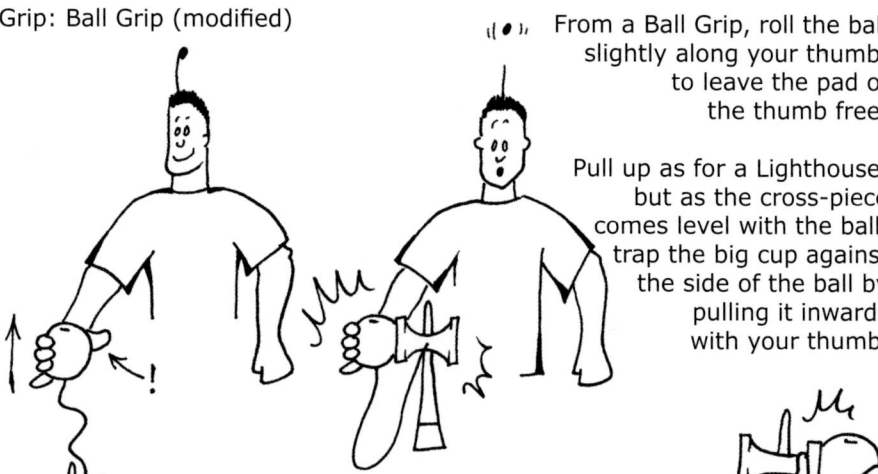

Exits
Hop up to a Lighthouse.
Half spin the ken into an Aeroplane catch.
Rotate the ken 180°, and re-trap the Small Cup.

Finger fun

Fork Catch (Fooku Kyatchi/フォークキャッチ)

Grip: Common Grip

This is a simple little idea which can look really effective when used as a way to link tricks together. From any cup or spike catch, gently toss the ball towards your free hand. Spread the index and middle fingers out in a 'fork', and catch the ball balanced on top of the fingers.

Return the ball to the ken in the cup of your choice.

Variations
Try Moshi Kame with a fork catch between each cup catch. You can even fork catch with the same hand that's holding the ken!

Bat (Koumori/こうもり)

Grip: Inverted Common Grip, rotated 90°

Start with the ken held as shown, with the lower edge* of the small cup horizontal.

*By "lower edge", we mean the one nearest to the base cup. So that's the one that's higher up in the picture then. Err... Hope that's cleared things up for you.

Dip down, then pull up and catch the ball leaning against the side of the ken, with the hole resting on the edge of the small cup.

Tip
Dip deep! It'll help to stop the ball turning on the way up.

Going bats

Bat Exits
(Koumori Kimariwaza/こうもり決まり技)

Grip: Inverted Common Grip, rotated 90°

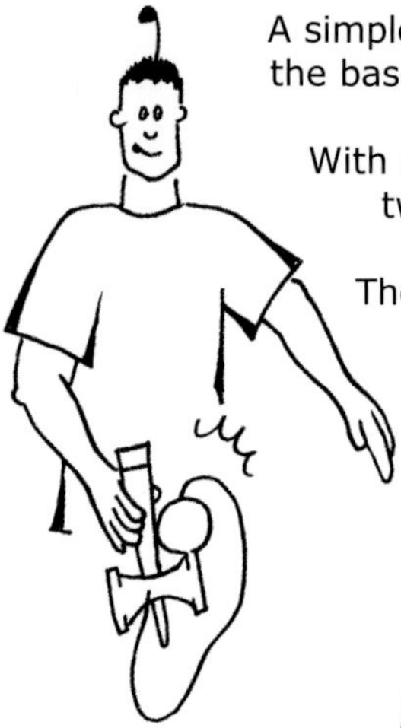

A simple exit from the Bat would be to just pop the ball up to the base cup. How about making it a bit more flashy though?

With a big knee-sink, throw everything up in the air, with a twist. Let the ken spin once, and catch it in a Pen Grip.

Then you should have just enough time to catch the ball on the base cup. You'll leave onlookers wondering what just happened.

Variation
If you throw so that the ken is pushed under and away from the ball, it's also possible to catch the ball first, then land an Aeroplane catch.

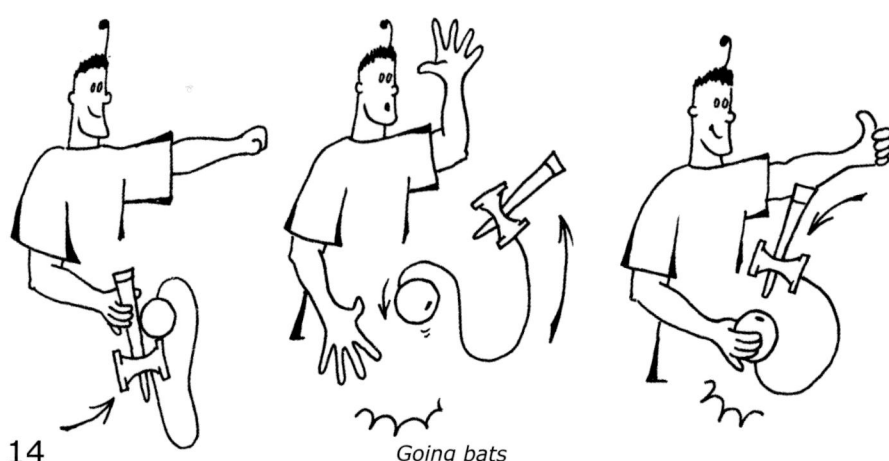

Going bats

Bat Turn
(Koumori Mawashi/こうもり回し)

Grip: Inverted Common Grip, rotated 90°

Bats and Birds fly around in the air, don't they? Well here's a couple of tricks to prove it.

After your Bat has roosted, relaunch the ball, giving a tug away from the ball as you do so. This will catch the edge of the cup in the hole, causing the ball to turn on the way up.

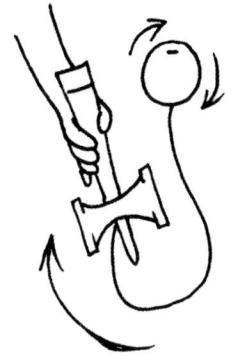

Now re-catch the ball back where it came from. Yes, this is a bit of a stinker!

Options
You can also spin the ball in the other direction, which is a harder launch, but means you can see the hole coming in to view as you attempt the catch. Or you can spin it at 90° to either of those planes.

Bird Turn
(Uguisu Mawashi/うぐいす回し)

Grip: Common Grip

Birds turn too. Exit a Bird with a sharp push forwards of the ken, to send the ball into a spin. Catch it back on the big cup edge.

Variations
Turn from Bird to Spike (Easier!)
Turn from Spike to Bird
Turn from big cup Bird to small cup Bird (and if you then Turn onto the Spike, that's Bird Turns Over The Valley)

Going bats

Falling Down (Saka Otoshi/さか落とし)

Grip: Ball Grip

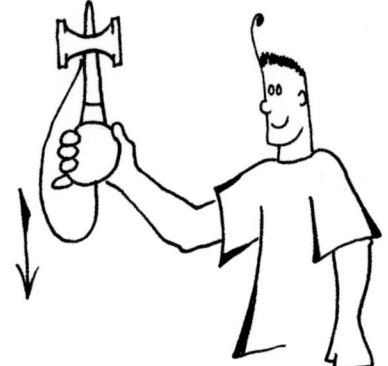

From the Lighthouse, re-launch the ken with a push of the arm and a staightening of the legs.

Keeping your eyes on the tip of the spike, drop down to an Aeroplane catch.

Tip
Don't try to give the ken too much rotation. The height of your re-launch should give enough time for it to turn gently by half a spin.

Variation
Let the ken spin one and a half times before the catch.

Sure, that's tricky, but we believe in you!

To the Lighthouse!

Tap In (Toudai Kaeshi/灯台返し)

Grip: Ball Grip

Start as you would for a Lighthouse, with a big dip before the launch.

As the ken passes the ball, give a *gentle* tap with the ball on the side of the base cup.

This should start the ken turning slowly, giving you enough time to drop down to an Aeroplane catch.

Tip
Keep your eyes on the tip of the spike.

Variation
Let the ken spin exactly once, and catch in a Lighthouse!

To the Lighthouse!

Build the Lighthouse (Touritsu/灯立)

Grip: Ball Grip

After landing an Aeroplane, re-launch the ken with a *gentle* flick of the wrist.

Half a spin is all that is required.

Keep your eyes on the base cup, and catch in a Lighthouse.

Faster Than Lighthouse (Iai Toudai/居合い灯台)

Grip: Ball Grip

They say every picture tells a story. These pictures tell the whole story!

Lift up, and use the string as an eye-guide.

Focus on the base cup, and swish down into a super-quick Lighthouse!

18 *To the Lighthouse!*

Lighthouse Somersault
(Toudai Tonbogaeri/灯台とんぼ返り)

Grip: Ball Grip

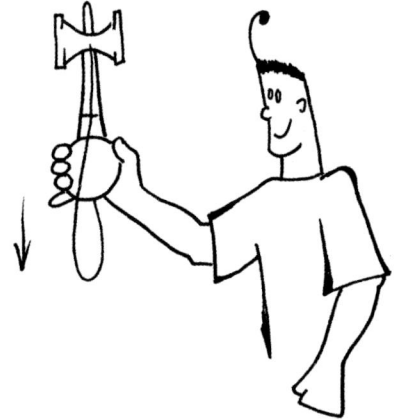

A Somersault trick is one where the ken starts off in a balance, is flipped 360° in the air, and caught back in the same balance it started in.

From a Lighthouse, push your arm forwards as you re-launch the ken. Use your knees to give height to the throw.

As the ken rotates in the air, keep your eyes on the base cup once it comes into view.

Catch back in a Lighthouse, sinking the knees initially, but pushing back up again to correct the balance if necessary.

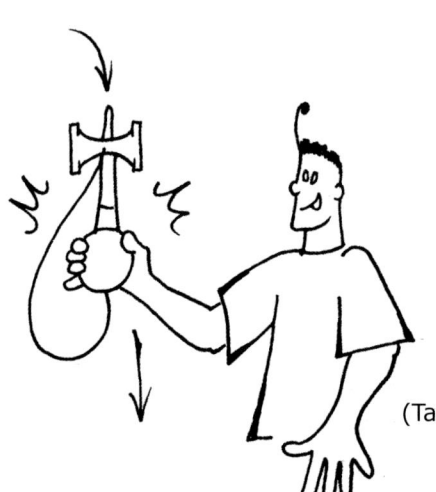

Difficult variations
2 spins? (Good luck!)

Moon Landing Somersault
(Getsumen Chakuriku Tonbogaeri/
月面着陸とんぼ返り)

Bamboo Horse Somersault
(Takeuma Tonbogaeri/たけうま陸とんぼ返り)

Transition from one ken-balance to another with a Somersault.

To the Lighthouse!

Reverse Swing In
(Ura Fuirken/うらふりけん)

Grip: Common Grip

This trick has the ball swinging up between your hand and your body, and onto the spike.

It's tricky, as there's no room for a full swing in the opposite direction to a normal Swing In, so we have to adapt the launch technique.

Launch as you would for a normal Spike, but at the same time, give a sharp push, diagonally up and away from you.

This will start the ball turning on its way up.

Now bring the ken back down below the ball, and catch it on the spike.

Tip
Watch the hole as it rolls over the top of the ball, trying to spot where to position the tip of the spike.

It's all coming back to me now

Reverse Aeroplane
(Ura Hikouki/うら飛行機)

Grip: Ball Grip

This trick works in much the same way as Reverse Swing In, but with the kendama the other way up.

Launch as you would for a Lighthouse, but give a slight forwards push with your hand as you do so.

As the ken rotates on its way up, try to keep your eyes on the spike.

Bring the ball under the ken, and let the spike fall down into the hole.

Tip
Try varying the amount and direction of the push, until you find the right combination.

Variations
By pushing a little harder, add an extra half spin for a Reverse Swing To Lighthouse, or an extra 1 turn for Reverse 1-turn Aeroplane.

(Look, it says "Variations", not "Easy Variations", okay?!)

It's all coming back to me now

Reverse Earth Turn
(Ura Chikyuu Mawashi/うら地球まわし)

Grip: Common Grip

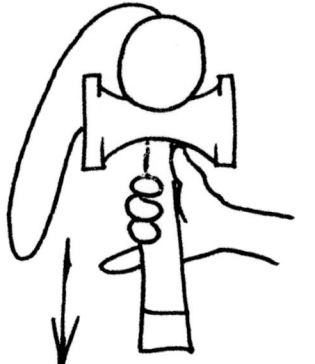

Start with a Reverse Swing In.

Re-launch using the knees, and as the ball starts to slide off the spike, tug the ken back towards you, keeping it vertical.

The tip of the spike should catch the ball as it is sliding off, sending it into a spin.

Catch the ball back on the spike after one spin.

Easier said than done, but again, try to watch the hole rolling over the top of the ball as a guide to where you should place the ken for the catch.

Variation
Sideways Earth Turn
(Yoko Chikyuu Mawashi/ 横地球まわし)
You've tried forwards and backwards, now how about turning the kendama on its side and doing an Earth Turn from there?

It's all coming back to me now

Jumping Stick Orbit
(Haneken Kidou/はねけん軌道)

Grip: Ball Grip

This one is relatively self-explanatory, but still a nice challenge. As you start a Jumping Stick, follow the forwards movement of your hand, into a large circle around the rotating ken.

If you complete your Orbit just quicker than the spin of the ken, then you can catch the spike back in the hole again, to the impressed gasps of your onlookers.

Variations
You can also do the Orbit in a different plane: across your body. This one looks better if viewed head-on.

If you feel like a real stinker of a challenge, why not try Lighthouse Somersault Orbit (Toudai Tonbogaeri Kidou/灯台とんぼ 返り軌道), or Moon Landing Somersault Orbit (Getsumen Chakiriku Tonbogaeri Kidou/月面着陸とんぼ返り軌道)?

Or for those who like to venture into the realms of the highly improbable, here's a Moon Landing Axle Orbit:

Is it even possible?!.....

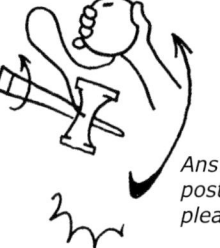

Answers on a postcard, please!

Yuri G would be proud

Captain Hook
(Hukku Senchou/フック船長)

Grip: Ball Grip

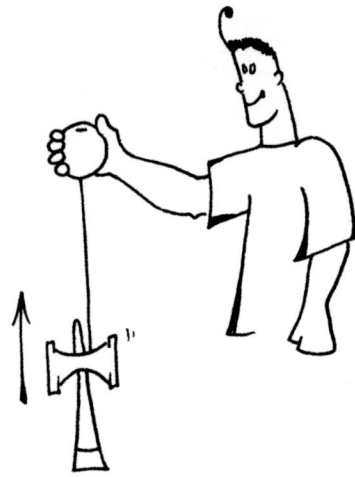

Begin with an upward launch as you would for a Lighthouse.

Stick out your index finger, and try to place it below the cross piece as it reaches the level of your hand.

Catch the underside of the Big Cup on top of the finger.

Exit by flipping the ken back up with a gentle half spin, and re-catch the spike in the hole.

Tip
You may need to let the base of the ken bump into your other fingers to stop it from tilting over, which would make it fall off the finger.

Variations
Enter the Captain Hook catch from a Jumping Stick throw.

Full spin exit to Lighthouse.

Or how about a somersault straight back into Captain Hook?

Or for the masochistic among you, exit to a Moon Landing.

Jumping Stick variations

Tomahawk
(Ura Haneken/うらはねけん)

Grip: Ball Grip

This is simply* a reverse-spin Jumping Stick, thrown from near the shoulder.

Use the knees to get good height on the throw, and if you're finding the launch tricky, think about pulling the ball away from the spike during the launch.

Watch out for the spike as it comes into view, and catch it in the hole.

Tip
Don't try to catch it too high - you'll probably need the 'fall time' to be able to spot the spike as it comes around.

One of those immensely annoying words, like "...just...".

Jumping Stick variations

Jumping Tapback
(Kometsuki Batta/米つきばった)

Grip: Ball Grip

Launch as for a Jumping Stick, but with very little spin.

Stop the ken spinning by letting the edge of the base cup hit the ball.

Now lower your knees and hand and try to catch the spike back in the hole.

This catch is quite tricky, as it's very hard to see where the spike is from this angle, so you'll need to use all your powers of judgement!

Tip
Don't tap the ken too hard, as you only want to stop the spin, not fully reverse it.

Variations
If, instead of stopping the spin of the ken, you tap more forcefully, you can send the ken into a full reverse spin before you make the catch.

Needless mental cruelty
Well, there's no reason to limit the scope of your ambition, so why not also try catching back into a Bamboo Horse?

Jumping Stick variations

Nodding Off (Kokkuri/こっくり)

Grip: Common Grip

After you're perched a Bird on the big cup edge, bend the knees, then re-straighten them, twisting the ken from a vertical to a horizontal position as you do so.

The edge of the cup should pull against the hole of the ball, causing it to tilt backwards, whilst *remaining in contact* with the ken.

Variation
Nodding On!
Come now, you don't really need me to explain this do you? You're a smart cookie, work it out.....

(Stupid cookies can turn to the bottom of page 32)

Sisyphus (Osuberi/おすべり)

Grip: Secret Grip

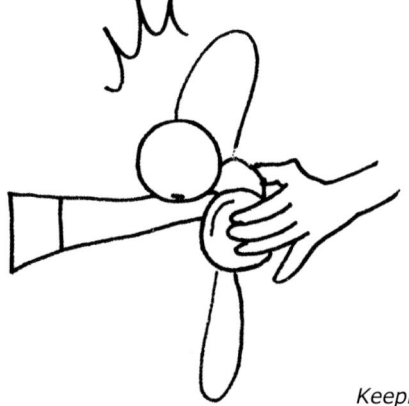

For those of you not familiar with Greek mythology, Sisyphus was a chap who was very good at rolling things uphill.

Pull up to a Body Catch, using the Secret Grip.

Keeping in touch

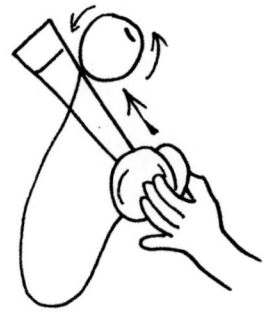

Using the ever-popular knee-dip, quickly rotate the ken from horizontal to vertical. This will make the ball start to roll up the slope of the ken, towards the base cup.

As the ball rolls over the edge of the base of the ken, it should 'pop' into place in the base cup.

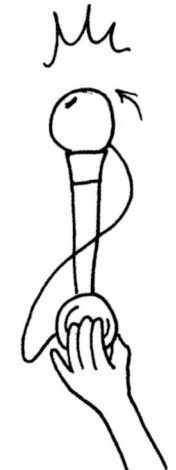

Tip
The ball should stay in contact with the ken for the whole time.

Exits
Reverse the procedure back to a Body Catch.

Or throw the ball up (with a little spin if necessary). Loosen your grip on the ken, letting it swivel downwards so that the spike is facing upwards, and catch the ball on the spike.

Swing Backhand Slip-on-stick*
(Furi Urakensaki Suberi/ふりうらけん先すべり)

Grip: Common Grip

Hold the ken in a common grip, with the spike pointing across your body.

Swing the ball up and across, gently tugging it as it approaches horizontal. Let the ball continue on its arc, and catch in a backhand side-spike position.

Now slide the ken back across your body, turning it as you do so, to slide the spike into the ball.

* Catchy name, huh?

Rolling Around (Ken Ookuri/けん大っくり)

Grip: Common Grip

Pull up and catch in a side-spike catch (as for Slip-on-stick).

With a twist of the wrist, and a gentle hopping motion of the knees, roll the ball around into the big cup.

The hole should now be facing away from you, and slightly upwards. So in a similar move to Nodding off, you can now roll the ball onto the spike.

Variation
You can practise just the last part of this trick to give you the feel for it.

That's Big Cup Slip-Stick
(Oozara Suberi/ 大皿すべり)

Rumble Strip

Grip: Non-standard Grip

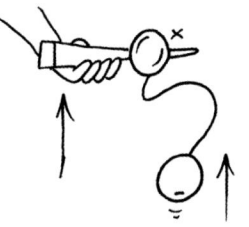

Keeping the upper surface of the ken clear, lift as if landing for a slip on stick.

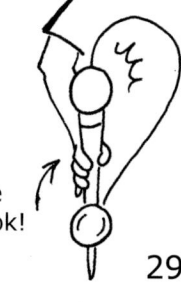

As it lands, sweep the ken under the ball, giving a lovely triple click, then catch to base cup. Once you have the timing, it's at least one of the best *sounding* tricks in the book!

Keeping in touch

Whirlwind Big Cup
(Tsumujikaze Oozara/つむじ風大皿)

Grip: Common Grip

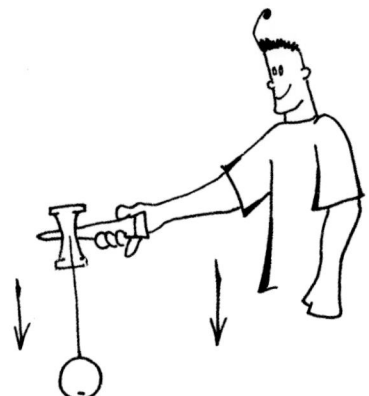

A "Whirlwind" trick is one where you throw the ken with one full spin and catch it again during the trick. Timing is everything for these tricks....

For a Big Cup Whirlwind, launch for a big cup catch, but with a little more height than usual. As soon as the ball has started to rise, quickly throw the ken one full spin (think "snappy") and catch it again.

You should have just enough time to catch the ball back in the big cup.

Tip
First, practise just the whirlwind throw without trying to catch the ball.

When trying the whole trick, you might find the ball suddenly snapping back towards the ken.

This is because it has gone too far from the ken, and the string has tautened. Try to keep the ball close to the flipping ken.

Variations
Try a whirlwind between consecutive big cup catches.

You can also Whirlwind Spike, or Whirlwind Swing In.

In a whirl

Gunslinger Swing In (Huusha Furiken/ 風車ふりけん)

Grip: Modified Common Grip

Start as you would for a Swing In, but with your thumb resting on top of the big cup.

After you have made the tug to rotate the ball, execute a fast Gunslinger, getting the speed by using your thumb to start the movement with a flick.

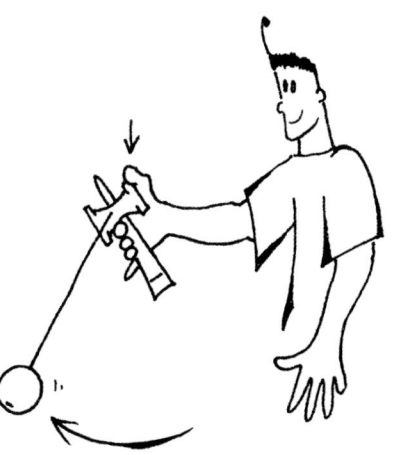

Now you have to catch the Gunslinger, move your eyes to spot the ball/hole again, and catch the ball on the spike. Easy, huh?

Tip
Okay, not so easy, as that last lot all happens very quickly, but as long as you make sure that wait to start the Gunslinger until *after* the tug, it should begin to seem possible after a few tries.

Variation
If you're feeling completely masochistic, try to drive the Gunslinger into a second rotation with your index finger before catching the ball!

More knees, etc...

In a whirl

Gunslinger to Balance
(Ganman Baransu/ガンマンバランス)

Grip: Non-standard Grip

Here's a tricky little move from The Mind Of Donald:

Try putting your thumb into the base cup as a Gunslinger comes round, and catching it in a balance.

Very satisfying when it works, rather destructive when it gets away from you.....

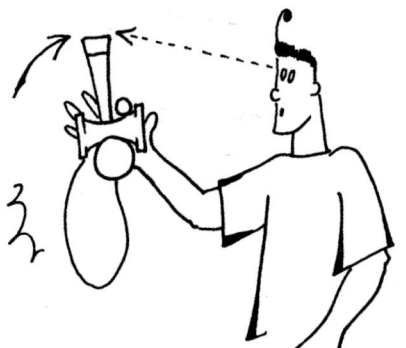

Warning
DO NOT practise this near anything breakable.

Don't say we didn't tell you....

Nodding On:
Same thing in reverse, dum dum!

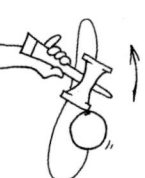

In a whirl

Lighthouse Baseball (Toudai Yakyuu/灯台野球)

Grip: Ball -> Pen Grip

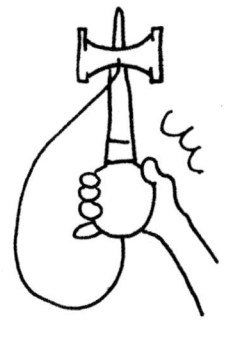

From a Lighthouse, drop the ball, and let the ken fall into a fork catch.

Now swing the ball in a full circle around the ken, changing to a Pen grip as you go.

Finish off by swinging up to a catch on any cup.

Mini Whirlwind (Mini Tsumujikaze/ミニつむじ風)

Grip: Common Grip

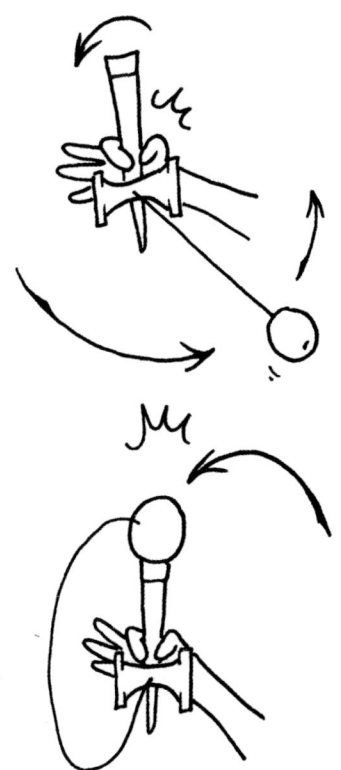

From a Big Cup catch, throw the ball up, and then very quickly give the ken a flicking throw up and towards you.

(Get a) Grip (on yourself)

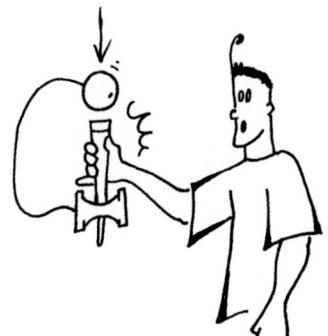

It should turn 3/4 of a spin.

Keep your eyes on the ken, catch it, and then catch the ball back on the base cup.

Cross-arm Turnovers
(Gyaku Mochikaewaza/逆持ちかえわざ)

Grip: Common & Ball Grip

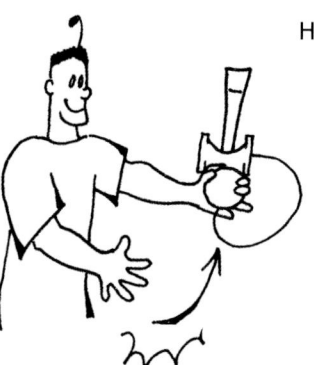

Here's a nice way of making a grip change look a little fancier.

Once you've learned the Apple and Jam Turnovers, try spicing things up by crossing your arms and swapping hands as you do them.

Tip
The passing arm can be either on top
or underneath.

Oh yeah, and "**knees!**"
of course.....

34   *(Get a) Grip (on yourself)*

1 Handed Fork Cradle
(Tebukuro Kyatchi/手袋キャッチ)

Grip: Non-standard Grip

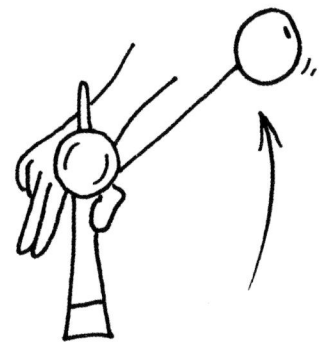

Hold the ken with index and middle fingers parallel to the crosspiece, small cup facing away from you.

Swing the ball to the left so the string comes around the small cup, around the fingers.

As it comes around the small cup the second time, release the ken and make a Fork Catch.

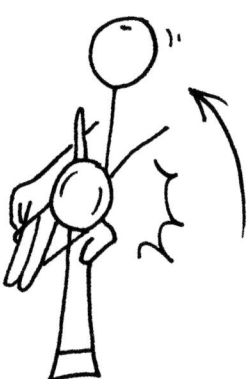

Variation
Try the same move, but with the string going round an extended little finger, rather than the other two. This leaves your other fingers free to catch the ball, and the cradle is easier to release as a flip to Aeroplane....

Rock the cradle

Gammon Trap
(Makisushi Oozara/巻き寿司大皿)

Grip: Non-standard Grip

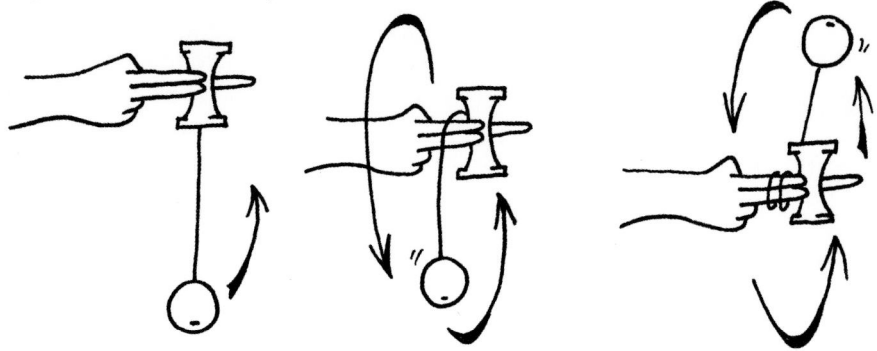

Hold the ken with your index and middle fingers parallel to the ken, fingertips on the crosspiece, big cup facing up.

Swing clockwise, with the string wrapping around both fingers and the ken body. If your string is regulation length (and why wouldn't it be?) then as the ball comes round the fourth time it should be almost wrapped up.

Now make the catch in the big cup, SPREADING YOUR FINGERS as you do. This should tighten up the slack, trap the ball in the cup, and allow you to relase hold of the ken entirely.

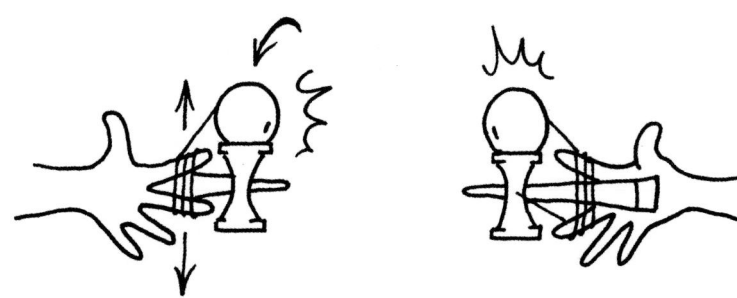

Rejected sequel titles:
As You Spike It
Tap Back in Anger
And No Birds Hang
On The Beech
Ruthless Tap Assassins
Click My Lovepump

The Sound and the Furiken
Bally-wood Dreams
Joseph and His Technicolour Heathcote
Kendama 2: Drilling for a Rainbow
More Knees! Beyond the Valley of the Kendama

Rock the cradle

Jumping Stick Cradle
(Haneken Ayatori/はねけんあやとり)

Grip: Ball Grip

Launch a Jumping Stick, and as the ken is spinning in the air, move your free hand's index finger forwards between the flying ken and the ball.

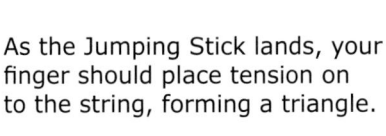

As the Jumping Stick lands, your finger should place tension on to the string, forming a triangle.

Now you can easily place the base cup onto the palm of the other hand, and the string tension will hold the kendama in a horizontal balance.

Exit
Turn your palm upwards, and gently throw the loaded kendama across to the other hand
(Where it started from!).

Rock the cradle

Double or Nothing Cradle
(Saradoumaki Oozara/皿どう巻き大皿)

Grip: Non-standard Grip

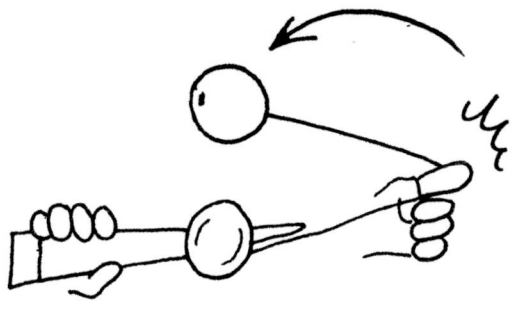

Swing the ball up towards your free hand, and let the string wrap around the index finger.

Allow the ball to keep on swinging, and the string to go around the cross piece, and back towards the index finger.

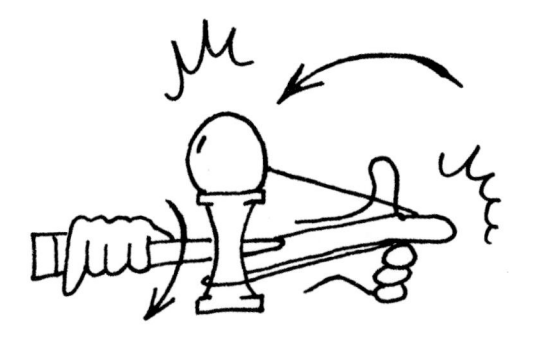

As the string wraps around the finger one more time, turn the ken so that the small cup faces upwards.

Catch the ball in the small cup.

Now you can place your thumb into the big cup, and let go of the ken entirely, going into a cradle balance on your other hand.

Now, wasn't that thumbthing special?

Exit
Gently 'throw' the whole kendama across to the other hand, (removing your fingers from the string) and catch it loaded in the big cup catch position.

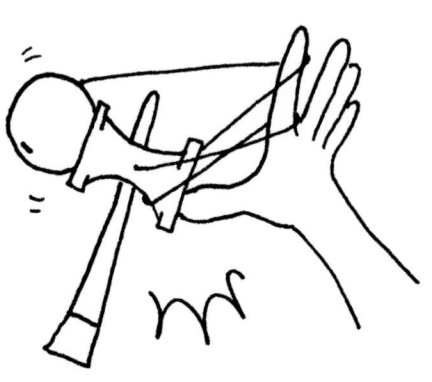

Rock the cradle

Stigmata

Grip: Common Grip (at 90°)

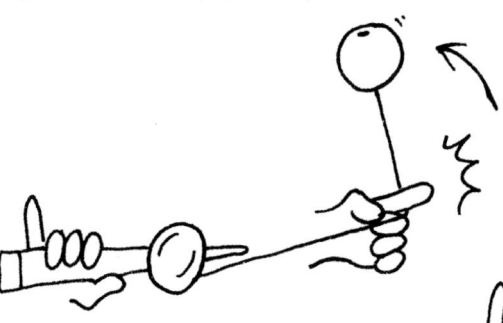

This one is similar in execution to Double or Nothing Cradle

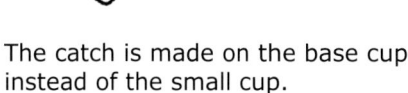

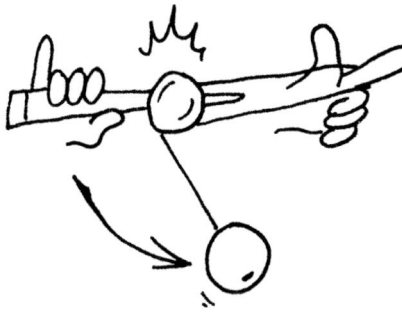

The catch is made on the base cup instead of the small cup.

There's not much spare string to play with, so bring your free hand quite close to the spike during the wrapping stage.

After trapping the ball on the base, place the spike into the palm of your free hand, then you can release the ken into a cradle balance.

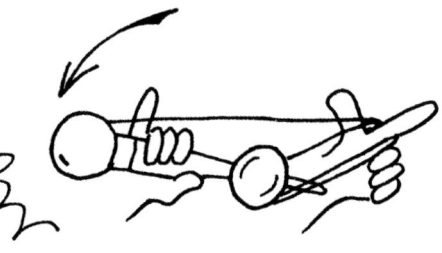

Exit
Throw the whole kendama across to the other hand, catching in either a Base Cup or a Candle position.

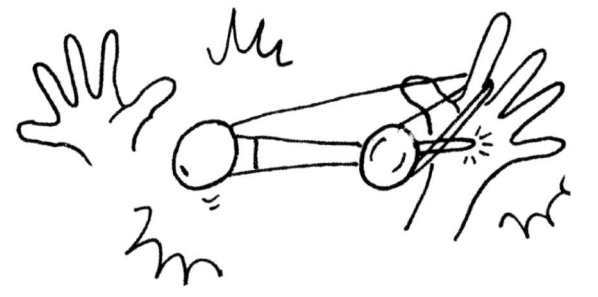

Rock the cradle

Extended Tap-backs (Ura Uchi/裏打ち)

Grip: Pen Grip

In a normal Tapback, the ken only makes a quarter-turn to do the tap. But with faster hands, it's possible to make a half-turn, and make the tap on top of the ball.

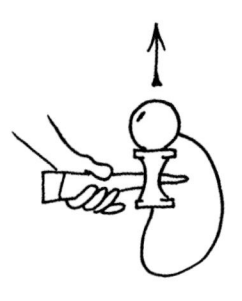

Tip
Make sure you're very gentle with your tap on the top! The ball should (hopefully) only be moving vertically.

Variation
A three-quarter turn to tap on the far side of the ball. With a very flexible wrist, and a high elbow, you can even completely circle the ball to tap underneath before you come back full circle to the catch.

Double Tap-back
(Nikai Maeuchi/二回まえ打ち)

Grip: Pen Grip

If you're quick with your tap-back, you can keep twisting the ken under the ball after the first tap, then tap again with the opposite side of the ken.

This second tap is upwards, from underneath the ball.

Then rotate back to a big cup catch.

Variation
Feeling fast? Try to get a third tap in there!

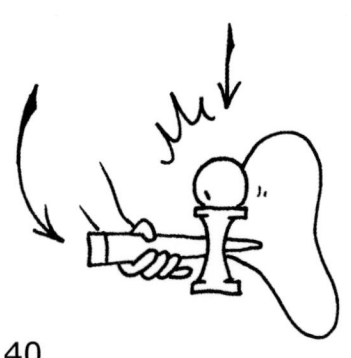

Tap dancing

Under Tap-back
(Hara Uchi/腹打ち)

Grip: Pen Grip

Also possible is to turn the ken 180° underneath the ball before you do the tap.

This is good practice for getting in the third tap mentioned above.

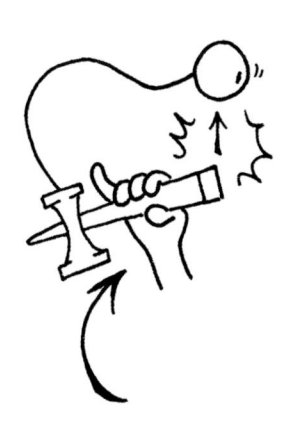

Stopover
(Muunsaruto/ムーンサルト)

Grip: Pen or Common Grip

Start with an index finger extended on your free hand.

Swing the ball up towards it, letting the middle of the string hit the underside of your finger.

The momentum of the ball will make it swing around your finger, towards the upper cup.

(You can use either of the cups on the cross-piece, depending on how you hold the ken.)

Tap dancing

As the ball hits the cup, lower both hands
and bend your knees to absorb the momentum.

Switch-hand Stopovers
(Ryoute Muunsaruto/両手ムーンサルト)

Grip: Pen or Common Grip

Think "Swap and Pop", but with Stopovers,
instead of cup catches.

Repeat on each side until you
get bored. Twenty or thirty
times should do it.

What do you mean, *"Is that it?!"* ?
Just look at the pictures....

On the other hand...

Stopover Tap-backs
(Muunsaruto Tataki/ムーンサルトたたき)

Grip: Pen or Common Grip

Swing the ball out of the cup to exit the Stopover, pinching the string between two fingers on your free hand.

As the ball swings under the ken, turn it so the base cup faces downwards. Then tap the ball sharply with the base cup, sending it swinging back up into a Stopover.

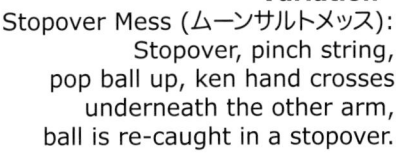

Variation
Stopover Mess (ムーンサルトメッス): Stopover, pinch string, pop ball up, ken hand crosses underneath the other arm, ball is re-caught in a stopover.

(The two triangles would form a bow tie shape if they both existed at once....)

On the other hand...

Around the Triangle
(Sankaku Isshuu/ 三角一周)

Grip: Pen or Common Grip

A sneaky little 3-stage trick.

Start with a Stopover, then pop the ball up by a few centimetres.

Keeping the string touching your index finger, move the ken towards your empty hand, but then very quickly back towards the ball, trapping the ball against the base cup. The string remains taut throughout this manoeuvre.

For the next stage, keep your eyes on the position of the hole. Pop the ball up again, with no spin, removing your finger from the string as you do so. Now quickly take the ken to the outside of the ball, then swish the spike into the hole, turning upwards at the same time.

(Looking smug: optional)

On the other hand...

44

Hanging Swing In
(Tsurushi Furiken/つるしふりけん)

Grip: Hanging Grip

Here's a Hanging trick that requires extra-fast hand movement.

Swing the hanging kendama away from you and up, releasing as you do so.

Immediately after you've released, move your hand up to catch the ken (in common grip). You should be trying to catch it before it has made a half-turn.

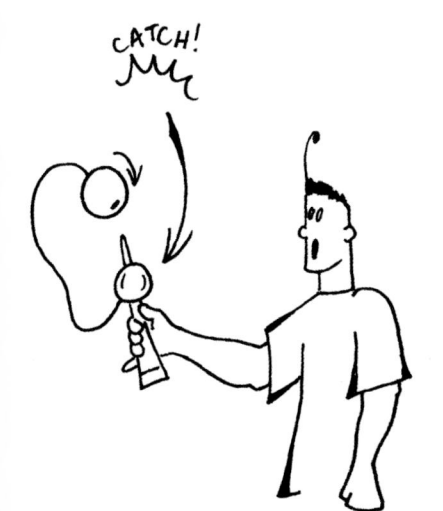

Now bring the ken back down below the ball as it carries on spinning. Watch for the hole rotating over the ball, and catch it on the spike.

Variations
Other Hanging tricks for you to try:
Hanging Big Cup
(Tsurushi Oozara/ つるし大皿)

Hanging Aeroplane
(Tsurushi Hikouki/ つるし飛行機)

Hanging 1-Turn Aeroplane
(Tsurushi Ikkaiten Hikouki/
つるし一回転飛行機)

Hanging around

Hanging Triangle Lighthouse
(Tsurushi Sankaku Toudai/つるし三角灯台)

Grip: Hanging Grip (modified)

I'm sure by now you can work out for yourself what a "Hanging Lighthouse" is, but here's a slight variation.

Start with the Hang as in the picture, balanced to form a steady triangle.

Pull up and slightly towards the 'ball side' of the string as you launch.

The ken should not move very far away from the ball (hopefully!).

Grab the ball while it is still moving upwards.

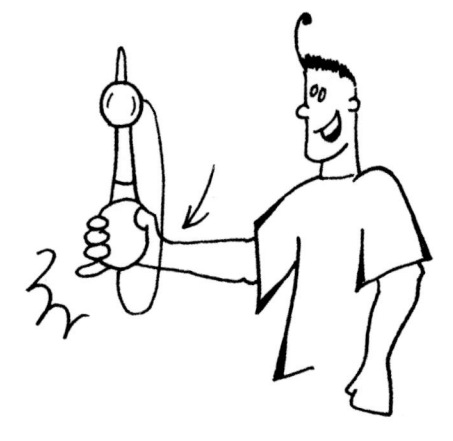

Catch back into a Lighthouse, just as the ken has tilted to an upright position.

Hanging around

The Drill
(Kirimomi/きりもみ)

Grip: Ball Grip

Start with a ball grip, with the ken 'loaded'. Use your free hand to give a sharp sideways spin to the cross piece.

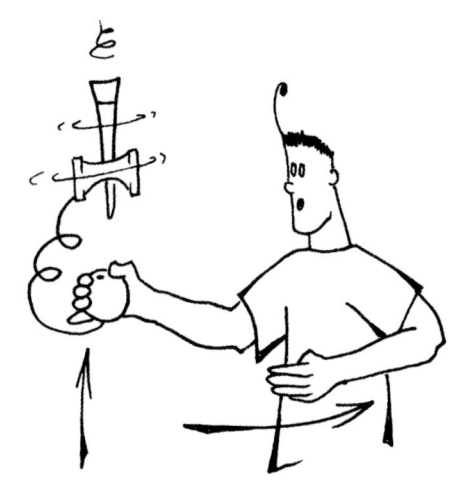

As you give the spin, straighten your legs so that the ken flies up out of the ball, spinning as it does so.

Keep your eyes on the tip of the spike, and sink back down to an Aeroplane catch.

Variation
Since you've got all that time while the ken is spinning in the air, why not amuse yourself by doing an Orbit in the meantime?

Defying classification

Sideways Drill
(Yoko Kirimomi /横きりもみ)

Grip: Ball Grip

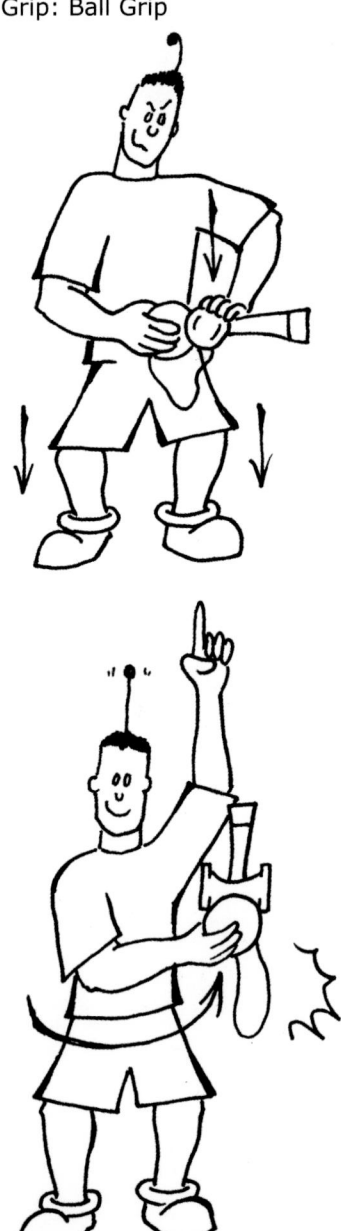

Hold the ball as you would for a Rotor Blade, and curve your free hand's fingers over the far edge of the cross piece.

Now spin the cross piece up and towards you, whilst at the same time taking the ball out to the side, and straightening your legs.

The ken should end up in a horizontal spin.

Now swoop the hole of the ball back onto the spike, twisting upwards as you go.

Tip
The recapture is the trickiest part.
If the ken's rotation is not perfectly straight, the tip of the spike will be spiralling around.

Try to get a nice clean release of the ball when launching the spin.

Defying classification

Fishing (Kozara Tsuri/小皿つり)

Grip: Common Grip

Donald writes:
" I've given these tricks the name of Fishing tricks, due to the fact that you hook them before you land them, ho ho... "

Lift straight up, as if for a Bird on the far (small) cup

Rather than catch, use the cup edge to hook into the hole while tapping upward, and pull back, to give the ball a reverse spin...

....whistle a happy tune in the intervening microseconds.....

...and Spike.

Variations
Once you've got that down, try the rest of the riverbank...

Bat Fishing (flip is easier, catch is nastier)

Base Cup Fishing, (Pen Grip & Common Grip)

Wingwalker Fishing

Defying classification

Landing Strip
(Ranuee/ランウエー)

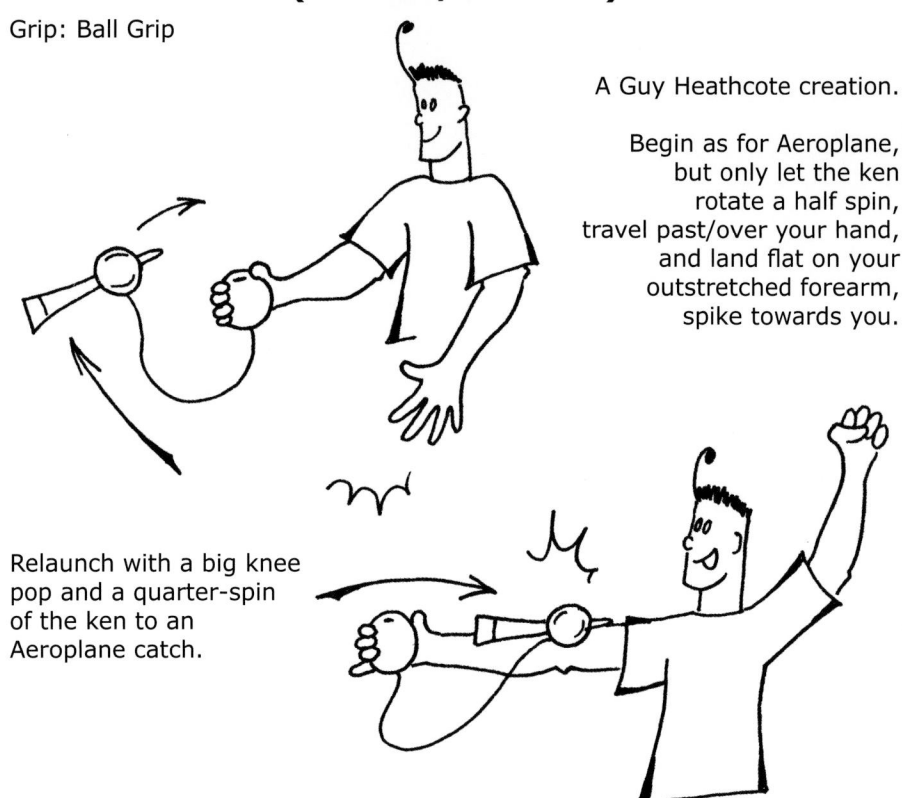

Grip: Ball Grip

A Guy Heathcote creation.

Begin as for Aeroplane, but only let the ken rotate a half spin, travel past/over your hand, and land flat on your outstretched forearm, spike towards you.

Relaunch with a big knee pop and a quarter-spin of the ken to an Aeroplane catch.

Alternatively let the ken make a full spin on the way up, and catch spike away from you, and re-launch to a Lighthouse.

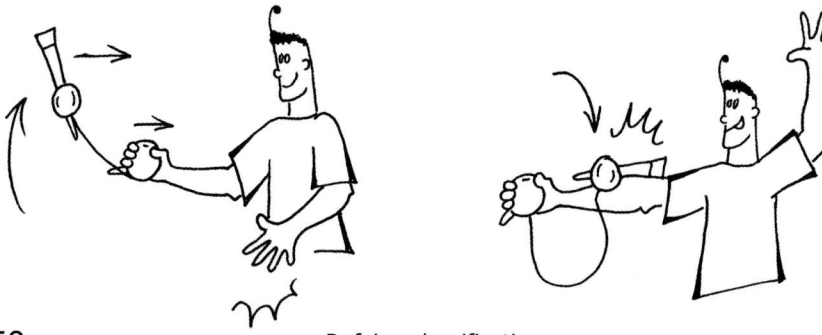

Defying classification

C-Whip (Surakku Hoippu/スラックホイップ)

Grip: Inverted Ball Grip

This is an adaptation of a diabolo "slack string" trick.

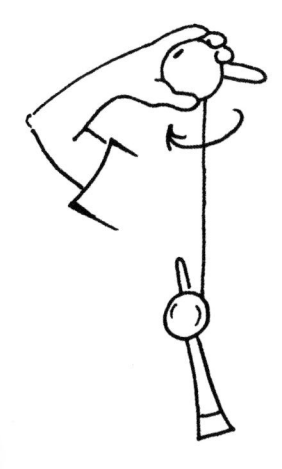

Hold the ball in an inverted Ball grip, and stick out your index finger. Rotate your finger clockwise (viewed from above) around the string. The ball hole should now be facing across your body, and your palm slightly upwards.

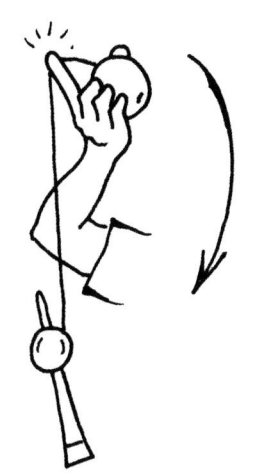

Now gently hop the hanging ken upwards, whilst very sharply drawing a fairly large capital letter 'C' in the air with your index finger. (Now you know where the name came from!) Your wrist and palm should rotate in/downwards as you do this.

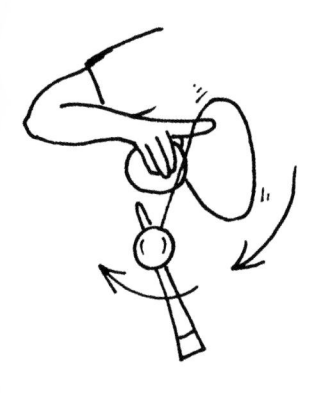

What should happen is that a loop of string should slacken, and travel over your hand and down towards the ken.

With a pinch of luck and a spot or two of practice, you should be able to get this loop to flick around the big cup. You'll then find yourself in a 1-handed cradle.

The simplest exit is to simply swap index fingers in the loop, then flick up to an Aeroplane catch.

There are more complicated exits too, but we'll let you discover those for yourself!

Defying classification

Elbow Drop
(Hiji Otoshi/肘落とし)

Grip: Common Grip

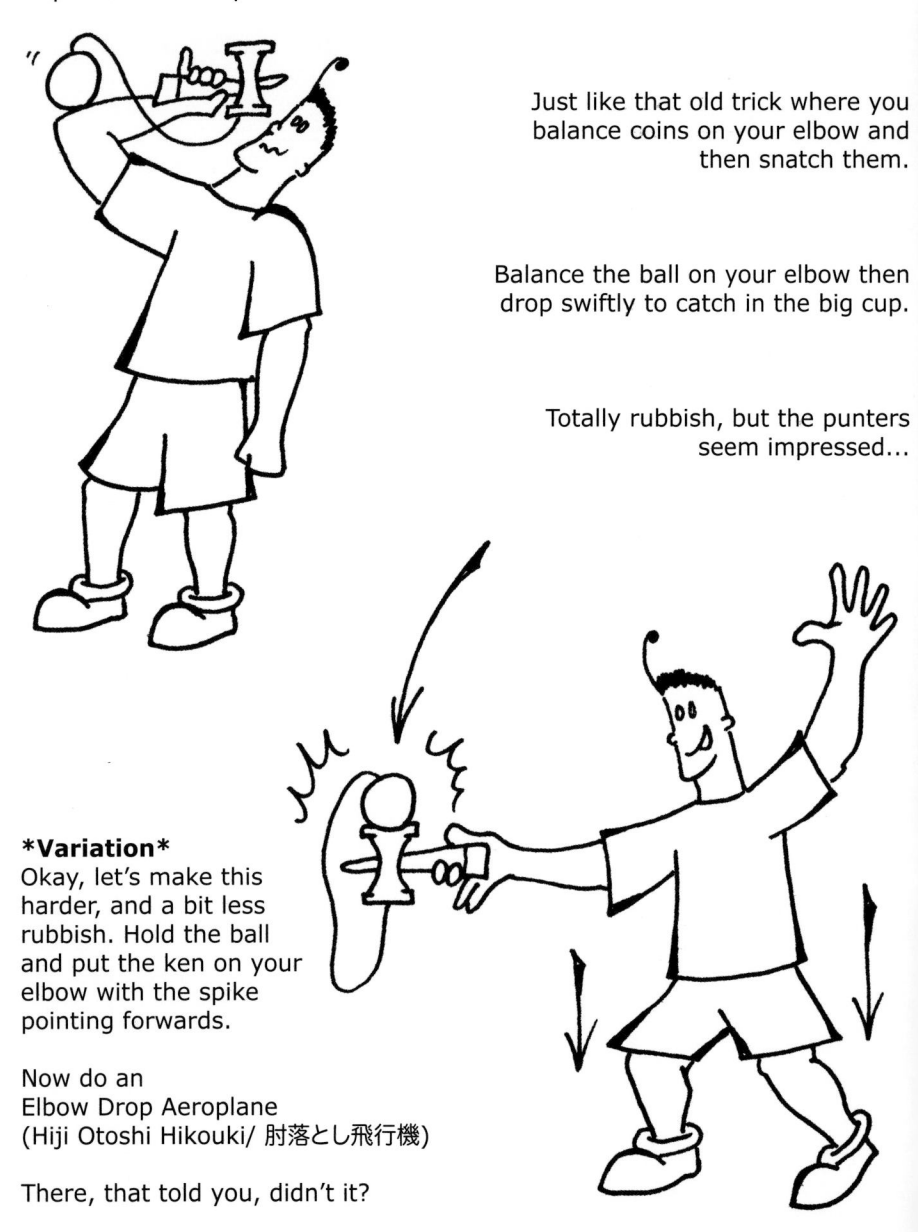

Just like that old trick where you balance coins on your elbow and then snatch them.

Balance the ball on your elbow then drop swiftly to catch in the big cup.

Totally rubbish, but the punters seem impressed...

Variation
Okay, let's make this harder, and a bit less rubbish. Hold the ball and put the ken on your elbow with the spike pointing forwards.

Now do an
Elbow Drop Aeroplane
(Hiji Otoshi Hikouki/ 肘落とし飛行機)

There, that told you, didn't it?

Defying classification

Mini Suicides (a.k.a. Mini Spacewalks)
(Han Uchuu Yuuei/半宇宙遊泳)

Grip: Ball & Common Grip

Hold the ken in the common grip, and swing the ball up to the side, so that it peaks when the string is horizontal.

Just as it gets there, give a sharp tug to the side, also releasing the ken. Move your hand across to the approaching ball, and catch it (as gently as you can).

Let the ken swing underneath the ball, and up to horizontal. Now you can repeat the procedure as many times as you like, alternating between catching the ken and the ball each time.

Exit
Finish off by catching the ken, and coming up to a catch on any cup, or onto the spike. Alternatively, finish with a ball catch, to an Aeroplane finish.

Suicidal tendancies

Suicide Swing In (a.k.a. Moon Circle)
(Engetsu Sappou/円月殺法)

Grip: Common Grip

The launch for this trick is just the same as for Suicide Aeroplane, but with slightly less sideways motion.

Use your knees to give plenty of height to the throw.

The catch will feel slightly awkward the first few times you try it, as the ball is still carrying the kendama upwards. For the catch you need your upper arm horizontal, forearm vertical, palm facing forwards, thumb opened and forwards, fingers upright.

Catch the ken back in a ken grip, but as gently as you can, since you don't want the 'jerk' of the catch to interrupt the flight of the kendama.

After you catch the ken, allow the ball to continue its upwards trajectory, up and over your hand, and out to the side. Now bend your **Knees!** again as the ball swings under your hand and across your body.

Straighten up as it starts to rise, and finish by tugging the ken to send the ball turning onto a spike catch. This second set of knee bends is really important for controlling the ball's path at the end.

Suicidal tendancies

Fast Hand Base Cup
(Hayate Chuuzara/はやて中皿)

Grip: Ball & Common Grip

An alternative exit to Aeroplane is to lift the whole kendama upwards, launching with the knees.

Grab the ken while it is still travelling upwards, and quickly scoop underneath the ball just before it starts to fall.

Catch in the base cup with plenty of 'sink'.

Those hands were fast as lightning

Fast Hand Lighthouse
(Hayate Toudai/はやて灯台)

Grip: Common & Ball Grip

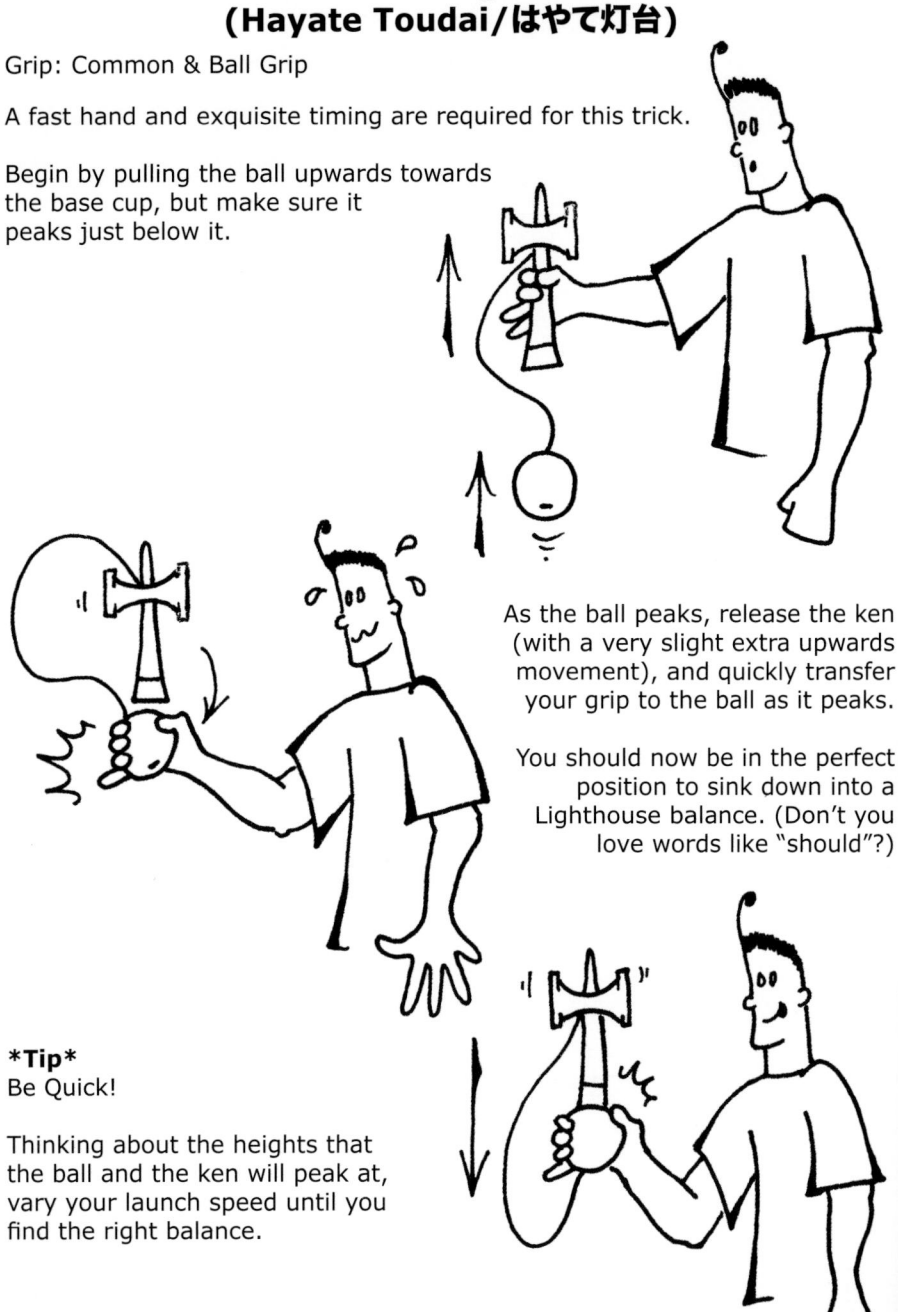

A fast hand and exquisite timing are required for this trick.

Begin by pulling the ball upwards towards the base cup, but make sure it peaks just below it.

As the ball peaks, release the ken (with a very slight extra upwards movement), and quickly transfer your grip to the ball as it peaks.

You should now be in the perfect position to sink down into a Lighthouse balance. (Don't you love words like "should"?)

Tip
Be Quick!

Thinking about the heights that the ball and the ken will peak at, vary your launch speed until you find the right balance.

Those hands were fast as lightning

Fast Hand Falling Down
(Hayate Otoshi/はやて落とし)

Grip: Common & Ball Grip

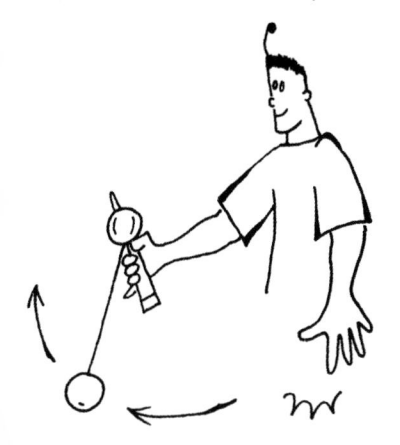

Begin as for Swing In. Wait until after the string has passed horizontal, then release the ken.

Now you have to be really fast, switch your eyes to the ball, and catch it in the ball grip.

Immediately release the tension on the string, and bend down to an Aeroplane catch.

Tip
At the launch, keep your arm a little further away from your body than normal. This will stop you from having to step backwards sharply to make room for the catch.

Matt Hall says
" Concentrate on keeping the tension on the string as you release. Also, release earlier than you think for a slower flip. "

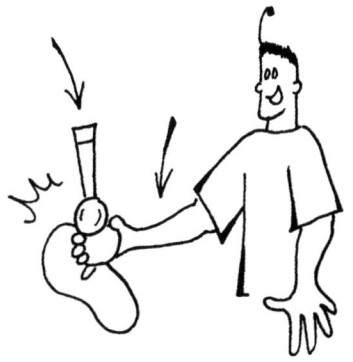

Those hands were fast as lightning

Orbit The World
(Sekai Kidou Isshuu/世界軌道一周)

Grip: Common Grip

Guy Heathcote writes:
" I have a moderately challenging sequence for you - Orbit The World. The idea is to do a regular Around The World, but do an orbit at each station. So, that's:

Small Cup, Orbit to Small Cup,
Big Cup, Orbit to Big Cup,
Base Cup, Orbit to Base Cup,
Spike,
Orbit around an Earth Turn.

Yes, it's the last one that's tricky, but so is keeping the string from getting wound up. "

One And A Half Times Two (Ikkaiten Hikouki Ikkaiten Touritsu/一回転飛行機一回転灯立)

Grip: Common Grip

Guy Heathcote continues his sinister kendama wizardry:
" Here's another trick sequence for you. Just two simple moves in this:

1.5 Aeroplane*, then 1.5 spin into Lighthouse.

I guess there could be a third element too '...Times Three': finish with another 1.5 into Falling Down, but this doesn't seem very likely.... "

* That's a "1-Turn Aeroplane", in which the ken actually turns 1.5 times. Confusing, huh?!

Around U.S.A.
(Beikoku Isshuu/米国一周)

Grip: Common Grip

A sequence from the twisted brain of Colin Sander, who casually describes it as " Around Europe with Earth Turns ". So that's:

Small Cup, Spike, Earth Turn,
Big Cup, Spike, Earth Turn,
Base Cup, Spike, Earth Turn.

Simple really. I don't know why we even bothered telling you about it.

Speed Trick B
(Taimu Kyougi B/タイム競技B)

This is the Speed List that the J.K.A. use in their Advanced ranking system.

Can you complete the tricks, in order, in under 2 minutes?
How about under 1?

See the British Kendama Association's website at **www.kendama.co.uk**
for more details on how to find out what your official skill level is!

1. Swing to Candle
(Mae Furi Rousoku / 前ふりろうそく)

2. Around the Prefecture
(Ken Isshuu / 県一周)

3. Around Japan 2 times
(Nihon Isshuu Nikai Renzoku / 日本一周二回連続)

4. Around the World 2 times
(Sekai Isshuu Nikai Renzoku / 世界一周二回連続)

5. Around Europe
(Yoropa Isshuu / ヨーロッパ一周)

6. Earth Turn
(Chikyuu Mawashi / 地球まわし)

7. Bird and In
(Uguisu-Ken / うぐいす〜けん)

8. Jumping Stick
(Haneken / はねけん)

9. One-Turn Aeroplane
(Ikkaiten Hikouki / 一回転飛行機)

10. Falling Down
(Saka Otoshi / さか落とし)

Around Tunbridge Wells
(Taanburijji-i Machi Isshuu/ターンブリッジ井町一周)

Jon Relf writes:
"In the world of the kendama there are a number of *Around the something or other* tricks, which involve the ball doing a sequence of tricks in order.

The Void told me about Around the USA, which I was very pleased to land after surprisingly few attempts. I showed off the trick at Tunbridge Wells Juggling Club recently & it was generally judged to be quite ridiculous. However, I think we can get more ridiculous.

So lets start with a simple list of moves:

Big Cup, Small Cup, Base Cup, Spike,
...are all self explanatory.

Penguin Base Cup:
-Catch the ball in the base cup with
the ken held Penguin style

Earth Turn:
-Flip the ball from the spike so it completes one turn,
 then catch back on the spike

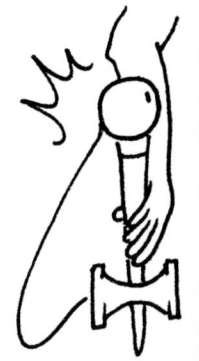

A "Penguin" catch

Then using my trusty Combination Generator we can generate a list of combinations from every location to every location. After a bit of trimming of all the same-to-same location throws & sticking in some Earth Turns to round off each section I now present Around Tunbridge Wells!

A mere 57 move sequence guaranteed to give your wrist a phenomenal workout. Can I do this trick? Of course not! After an hour & a half worth of trying, I managed to complete each section individually apart from the Earth Turns. But the furthest I've got through the whole list is to the Small Cup in the Penguin Base Cups section.

Start by holding your kendama in a Common Grip with the ball hanging down, then work your way through the list, & remember...

"It's all about hole control" - Matt Hall

A. The Big Cups:
1. Big Cup
2. Small Cup
3. Big Cup
4. Base Cup
5. Big Cup
6. Penguin Base Cup
7. Big Cup
8. Spike
9. Earth Turn

B. The Small Cups:
10. Small Cup
11. Big Cup
12. Small Cup
13. Base Cup
14. Small Cup
15. Penguin Base Cup
16. Small Cup
17. Spike
18. Earth Turn

C. The Base Cups:
19. Base Cup
20. Big Cup
21. Base Cup
22. Small Cup
23. Base Cup
24. Penguin Base Cup
25. Base Cup
26. Spike
27. Earth Turn

D. The Penguin Base Cups:
28. Penguin Base Cup
29. Big Cup
30. Penguin Base Cup
31. Small Cup *
32. Penguin Base Cup
33. Base Cup
34. Penguin Base Cup
35. Spike
36. Earth Turn

E. The Spikes:
This section is similar to Around Europe but with the extra penguin catch.

37. Big Cup
38. Spike
39. Small Cup
40. Spike
41. Base Cup
42. Spike
43. Penguin Base Cup
44. Spike
45. Earth Turn

*This is as far as I've got!
- Jon, July 2010

**This is as far as I've got! Argh!
- Void, March 2011

F. The Earth Turns:
This section is similar to Around the USA but with the extra penguin catch.

46. Big Cup
47. Spike
48. Earth Turn
49. Small Cup
50. Spike
51. Earth Turn
52. Base Cup
53. Spike
54. Earth Turn
55. Penguin Base Cup **
56. Spike
57. Earth Turn***

***If you got this far you rock!"

Sequences

Sequences

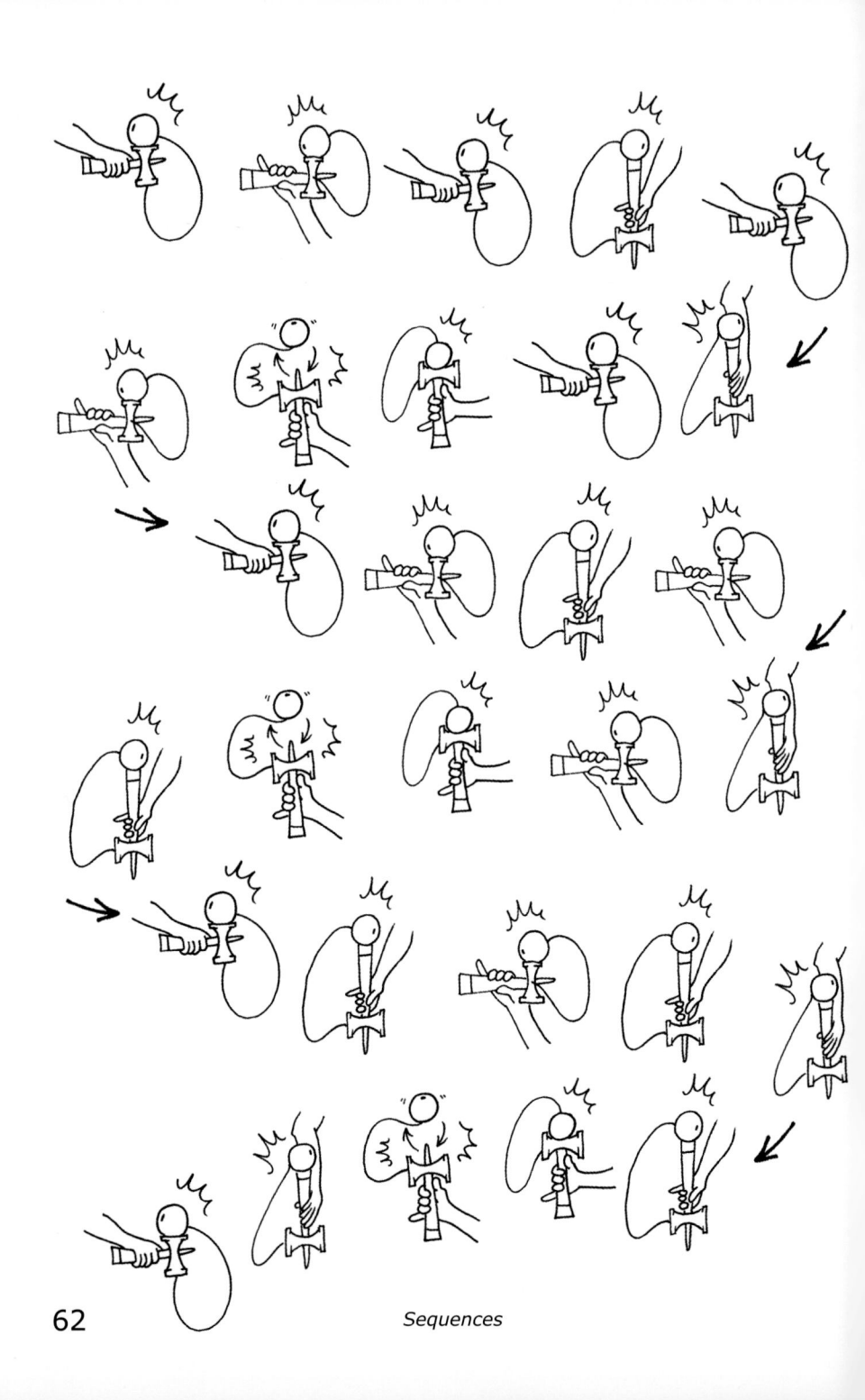

Sequences

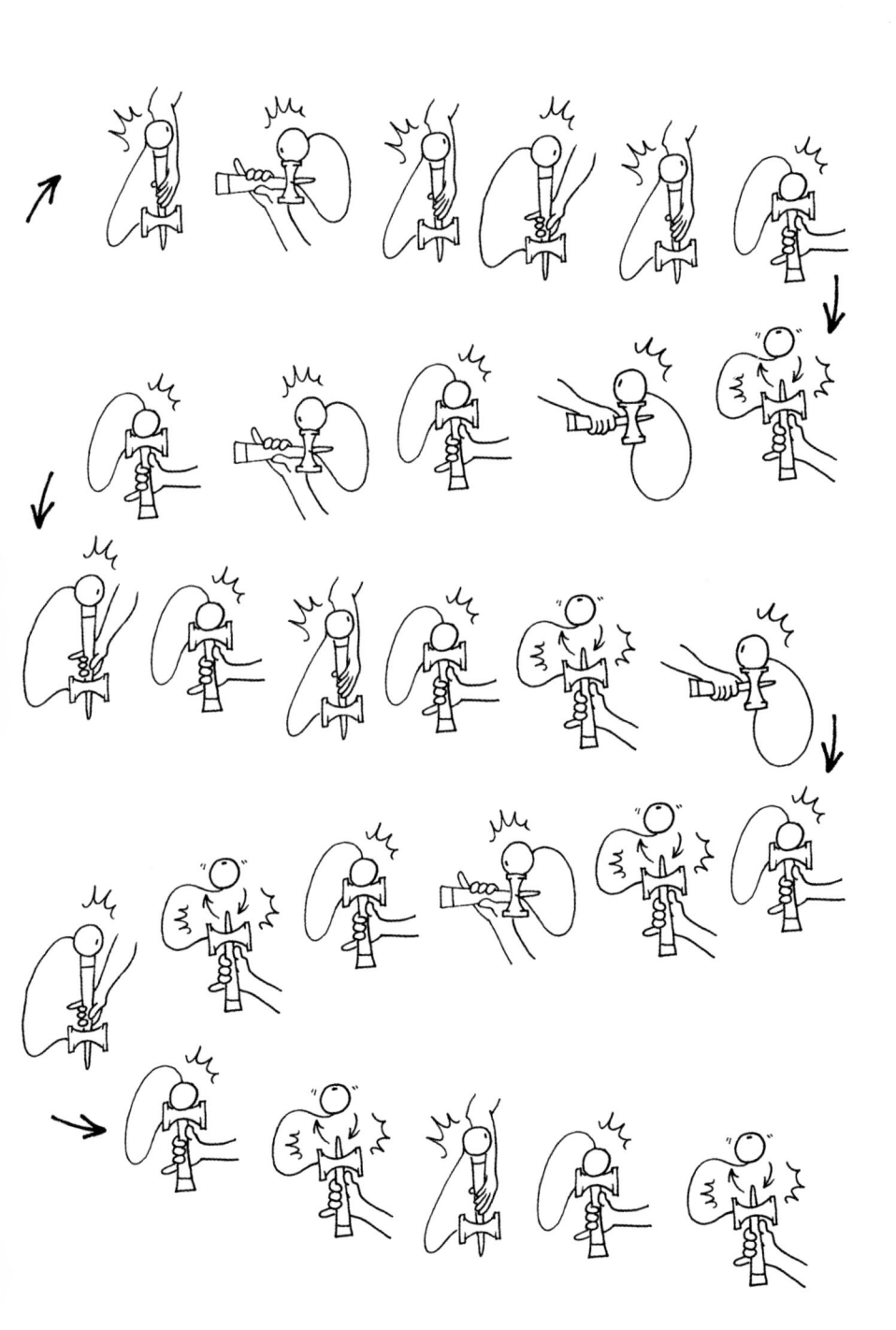

The Last Word

"Have you noticed that whatever sport you're trying to learn, some earnest person is always telling you to keep your knees bent?"
-Dave Barry

Thank You

Matt Hall, Laurie @ Butterfingers Books, Guy Heathcote, Matt Pang, Tom Derrick, Robin Gunney, Arron Sparks, Jon Relf, David Marchant, Gabi Keast, Stewart Hutton, Matt Ledding, Colin Sander, Jeffrey Van Reeven, Mr Jumpshoe, Kendamatty, Samuli Männistö, Peter Bergmann, K CIMA, Yusuke Ito, www.juggling.tv , and all the players who've helped to make the British and European competitions a success.